S0-AQM-246

Red as a Lotus

RED AS A LOTUS

letters to a dead trappist

Lisa Gill

LA ALAMEDA PRESS   ALBUQUERQUE

Thanks to the editors of the following publications where poems from this series have appeared: *The Harwood Review, the rag, Vox Populi, The Weekly Alibi, Anthology of New Mexico Poets 1960-2000*. Thanks also to visual artist Valerie Roybal and Utility Press for incorporating one of these poems in the design and creation of 30 handmade artist's books. Muchas gracias to Mark Weber for recording poems from this series to include on VOL.3 of the *Albuʒerxque* CDs. Some poems first appeared in chapbooks by the author.

I am grateful to all of the friends and catalysts in my life, even when the two aren't synonymous. Special thanks must go to Mitch Rayes for introducing me to the work of Thomas Merton and for quoting the poetry of Jaime Sabines whenever I was in need; to the anonymous friend who sent Ernesto Cardenal's *Apocalypse and other poems* which includes the beautiful "Coplas on the Death of Merton"; and to J.B. Bryan for having faith in this book long before I began to think of it as a "book", and for his tremendous patience and support throughout the process. And finally, my profound gratitude to Thomas Merton (1915-1968) and love to my grandmother Vernice Landis (1910-2001).

All Rights Reserved

Copyright © 2002 by Lisa Gill

cover: Lotus Blossom—J.B. Bryan   *watercolor on paper*

ISBN: 1-888809-33-7

Library of Congress Cataloging-in-Publication Data

Gill, Lisa, 1970-
  Red as a lotus : letters to a dead Trappist / Lisa Gill.
    p. cm.
  ISBN 1-888809-33-7 (alk. paper)
  1. Merton, Thomas, 1915-1968--Poetry. 2. Spiritual life--Poetry. 3.
New Mexico--Poetry. I. Title.

PS3607.I443 R43 2002
811'.6--dc21

2002014347

La Alameda Press
9636 Guadalupe Trail NW
Albuquerque, New Mexico 87114

Cicadas & Other Background Phenomena

This is the kind of book that practically writes itself when you live alone in a little trailer next to an alfalfa field and are lucky enough to have a copy of Thomas Merton's *Seeds of Contemplation* on hand.

As he wrote, "The purpose of a book of meditations is to teach you how to think and not to do your thinking for you. Consequently if you pick up such a book . . . as soon as any thought stimulates your mind or your heart you can put the book down because your meditation has begun."

So I found myself writing to a Catholic monk, political activist, hermit and poet who died two years before I was born. And for over two years I kept writing. Although I continued reading works by Merton throughout the process, my task was personal.

Merton had been explicit: "Many poets are not poets for the same reason that many religious men are not saints: they never succeed in being themselves... They wear out their minds and bodies in a hopeless endeavor to have somebody else's experiences or write somebody else's poems or possess somebody else's sanctity."

Red as a Lotus is the natural result of accepting Merton's challenge, given the individual circumstances of my life. Admittedly, at times I felt as if I'd accidentally pried back the lid of Pandora's box. Yet, although these poems are not the ones I'd abstractly envisioned writing to Thomas Merton when I began the series, I'd have to say, nonetheless, that they are precisely the ones I needed to write.

Late last night I walked my dog into the alfalfa field. The moon was so bright that the big cottonwood's shadow was clearly demarcated. As my feet traced the line between light and dark, following the contour of a tree cast down into a field, I thought, "Here is the book."

Red as a Lotus is in your hands now.

LG

Alameda, New Mexico

"Two white butterflies alight on separate flowers.
They rise, play together briefly, accidently, in the air,
then depart in different directions."

THOMAS MERTON
The Asian Journal

Dear Thomas,

I write because we have something in common,
not death though that might work metaphorically,
rather what's in our chests: your sternum and
my sternum are so similar I find myself hopeful.
Perhaps life can be endured despite this nasty bone.
You managed to live, up until some shoddy electrical
connection finally got you. I'm still here, writing,
in a little trailer where everything is a short.
Blown fuses and fragile links make the flickering
I see the world by. God is bright and then dim
shifting every time I tap the wall. You can see why
I write you though I don't know your address.
Besides, I trust you wouldn't tell me to just *get over*
this wasteland, but instead, to go forth and map.

ii.

If I have stopped reading to write you,

it is only because you instructed me to do so.

The best books pry the brain open like a clam shell,

lobes on each half skull and there, in the middle,

not simply a pearl but the corpus collosum,

a whole ocean for divers to plumb. I hold my breath

and flail my arms. Everything and my face is blue.

A bird flapping makes me gasp. I shall choke

on sky Thomas and you will call me *the absurd one*

shake your head and begin listing the names of

fishermen until I stop thinking of drowning and

remember wood, the possibility of a canoe, how breath

continues without consent, and lungs are nothing but

strange disobedient fish taking in what comes along.

iii.

So if it's true as you suggest that despair
is the epitome of selfishness then I am a queen
who'd quickly hide her face in shame if it wasn't
already embossed on coins in other people's pockets.
My question is simple. What if some medicine can
dethrone me? Would you have me nonetheless cling
to all my failings with hard fists, keep wringing
this bad brain out and hanging it on a line from
the old testament or one of your books to dry while
behind each sunny front comes a wailing typhoon?
Or rather, should I start from some freshly muddled
place, a slightly less original sinner with average
attachments to overcome before taking up the already
quite impossible task of good contemplation?

iv.

Ever hop a train? I haven't. Any aspirations
to travel derailed long ago with the daily grinding,
but conversations always feel like train rides as
words become windows where we view the world
and our own reflections. Whenever the talk stops
it's a whole new landscape. I don't always like
where I get left off. My feet get sore from thinking.
A friend who rode the rails north from Mexico
said people were looking for *chamba. Esclavitud.*
Slavery. Did I tell you I'm unemployed right now?
That's my slang for sick. As I sink deeper into poverty
I remember you wrote of two kinds: one common humble
back bent to a field or prayer, the other stooped to breaking.
When I recover, I'll search for work. Remember me.

V.

Up there in your big contemplation in the sky
do you know what I'm doing? Right now? How
I smoke cigarettes, write poems, and drink water
with a swig and a lip smack and a pretended swagger
as if it were wine. As if wine could be enough.
It was not my choice to derive so little satisfaction
from the pleasures that even you say God put here
for pleasing us, the same ones you freely revoked
in search of something higher. My heart's small
intuition has always held out. I haven't known
what to think of myself. When I pull solace
from your pages to wipe my brow, I admit I feel
less like a freak, as if indulging in ink was a form
of communion, one beetled brow knit unto another.

VI.

You were never able to kick the poet all the way out
onto the back stoop with the stray cats, were you? One
chamber of your heart remained a smoke-filled cafe
held open for the rest of us afflicted. As if your innards
rose up through your throat and persisted in making
your mouth full of letters and images even as your body
did the daily work of the monastery. If every odd tree
fulfills the great design of a ditchbank, and people
are no more than odd trees with free will, then even
the yakking can be transformed and serve some unseen
purpose. So, here is my mouth. The cavities in my teeth
are growing. Each small fracture has a chance, if slim,
to crack large enough to hold a mustard seed. Then,
hope or some wild plant shall take over my tongue.

vii.

Almost fifty years ago a novice in a convent had a vision.
God told her to leave and have a family. So she married
the man she'd left for Christ and kept small vigil over coffee
and casseroles in the kitchen. If her firstborn attended school
on his knees—because he could—zeal was the least of what
went unchecked. But despite deals he made in Detroit, his ears
remained bent, perhaps to his mother's faith, or maybe just
wrenched out of whack by nuns' reprimands. Later he gave up
scholarships, took his Bible, and after returning home to borrow
books from his mother, stuck his thumb out and hitched south.
In New Mexico he crossed paths with a woman who was thinking
too much and looked it. He told her, *even fools deserve teachers*,
and loaned me seeds. Years later contemplation sprouted.
It was a miracle you knew well enough not to doubt or predict.

viii.

I watched the lunar eclipse. Ever so gradually the shadow
of the earth crept across the surface of the moon until nothing
but an infinitely fine sliver remained. And standing under
a street lamp, I realized I'm part of what blocks the light,
just another person on this planet spinning about, following
one dizzying pattern after another, rarely bothering to calculate
the ramifications of my orbit. Perhaps despite every attempt
to move in good faith, I'll always end up coming between the sun
and the place it should shine. When the moon started waxing,
people spilled back into buildings. I held out, thinking how
fifteen minutes ago, the bars emptied onto the street and
for a while, we all stood still and looked up, past any neon,
to the moon—as if it were new, as if it were last call. Heading
back into the bar I prayed my shadows shed such light.

ix.

Outside there is so much water in the air, anyone
can forget drought though the earth stays bone dry.
Illusory relief. A strong wind could knock you down
into nothing other than dust, and fire is as much a threat
as ever. For a moment however, something was quenched
and a person wants to take this dampness to heart. I do.
I am tired of being parched, of looking in the mirror
only to see another barren landscape given over to sand
and sagebrush. Back inside I do the dishes, zealously,
wet from hand to elbow, but water's not the solace,
work is. I take the rag to the dishes as if my compunction
were stuck to the bottom of a cup and could be forced
loose. When I throw the dishwater out the back door
the desert will still be there but I won't wish for rain.

X.

Fear is such a funny thing. I try to see things the way
you might, but for me trust is a vestigial organ, hardly
functioning at all. And though there's nothing I'd like more
than to give my rent bill over to God, I'm practical and
can't see how that would appease my landlord. Religious
order is not in my future, marriage even less likely, so
every day is a barrage of need: food, shelter, eyes and teeth.
I rip into my limits and work, try to search out a community.
At best I am a misfit, some days a pariah, outside hope,
beating my fists on all these questions. Moses should part
my thinking and lead me across this broken wasteland
to a place where I can take decent steps, one foot in front
of the other, simple work, walking finally on a path
that can lead me to some city other than destitution.

xi.

I have the same pig-shaped skull as most of the species,
a veritable phrenologist's dream, all knotted and lumped
into just about every large category of failure. I'm poor,
addicted to nicotine, sometimes self-destructive, kind when
it's convenient. And so stubborn. Did you know I can hardly
ask a person on the street corner for directions let alone God?
That's why I have to write to you. No offense, but you're not
really the only destination for these letters. You're kind of
an intermediary, what some would call an intercessor, between
the me all flubbed up that I am now and what's possible.
Outside of this brain is the big everything. I would like to hold
life tight against my grey matter as if we were lovers. Once
I banged my head and got a concussion. I'd like to bang it
again and get clarity. Your books are rocks. Stone me.

xii.

My father feeds the birds in the shape of a cross. Twice
each day common sparrows and a pair of morning doves
rut over the six foot splay of seed in dirt that's bricked off
from the sod for this express purpose. I have to say
his backyard iconography is awe-inspiring, a living
chirping flapping dirt-bathing crucifix. If you asked him,
he'd tell you he does it so God knows he's looking out
for the little ones. I believe that. I think he also knows
he's one of the little ones, like we all are, confronted
daily with big sky and unfamiliar lawns. His brain lays
patterns everywhere, as if sense can be made simply
by repetition. Across the yard grow twenty tomato plants.
Inside are hundreds of empty coffee cans and the freezer's
full of orange rinds because God is everything detailed.

XIII.

It surprised me to find out you weren't raised in the Church,
that you came from the same Catholic-fearing background
I'm from, and were able nonetheless to get to a monastery.
In childhood, I was many shades of Protestant, taught early
that Catholics were going to hell. My best friend in grade school
was Catholic only because of when she was born. Her parents
had made a deal. The father got dibs on deciding the first kid's
religion while the mother got the second. When I learned that,
we were playing, trying to get to heaven on hopscotch, and right
there, I was struck by the terrible randomness of the God we get.
I'm still struck. Back then I had enough respect of differences
that conversion never crossed my mind though I actively grieved
my friend's anticipated damnation. Now, afterlife is the least
of my concerns. Life though, looms large and formidable.

XIV.

When I got food stamps, I also started getting my period more
regularly. That's a bit blunt and I'll admit this connection between
blood and grocery stores surprised me. I'd been eating something
all along, at least lately, so I didn't expect that simply having a little
more food stocked in the trailer would make such a difference. (Can
I still make you blush, Thomas?) Life is filled with strange accidents
of cause and effect and I can't help looking for understandings that
might make my day easier, whether it's common sense or God or science.
Maybe this means nothing to you, but, for me, this is about bones.
The women in my family break hips. When we read Genesis, our ribs
crack. Each fracture points towards a metamorphosis: we are becoming
birds. Daily I crane my neck and all my hollow vertebrae skyward,
wondering when I'll fly, wondering why I can't already. Probably
the answer is obvious: a lack of feathers or faith or calcium.

XV.

Church on Sundays was standard when I was a child but
bad weather made the best chapel. During storms, we'd stay
home, sitting on the edge of the bed with a Bible, a hymnal,
and curtains open just in case any sun might break through.
I was enamored of this time with my mother and brother,
my father sometimes poking his head in to yowl a refrain.
These days I don't go to any services and as for thunder,
I weather it alone. Rain on tin is loud. I can hardly think
so I sit still, light a candle, and listen. Sermons crop up
everywhere. Last season grasshoppers plagued my garden.
A week ago I bellied up in a whale of a misunderstanding
with a friend. Tonight I went outside with the dog and
a star shot across the sky as if pointing to the alfalfa field.
Things are simple. I walk in the north valley and fear no evil.

XVI.

One of my grandmothers got caught reading the newspaper
upside down. Can you blame her? What's written there makes
you think the whole planet's topsy turvy, yet most of us
only blink at poverty and murder and war because we have to,
closing our eyes is involuntary. My grandmother though, she tried
to turn the entire world on its head and instead got carted right off
to doctors. They operated to remove a brain tumor and fix her
world view. During surgery my father surmised God would let
his mother live when he saw the sky change colors. And she did live,
though I suspect he only saw what happens most days, a sunset
or a sunrise, which makes me wonder if it takes some sort of lesion
for this species to see what's really going on. Perhaps my grandma's
skewed vision, corrected like a straying sheep, was an opportunity
for all of us to reassess what we find so right-side-up in this world.

XVII.

The month I tried following the liturgy of the hours, I was
as always, being tossed by moods, the world from my eyes
wildly changeable. So this was about the clock, more than God,
about days and weeks and my desire to weave at least a single
thread of consistency through them, to make a tapestry, however
palely designed, out of my mish mosh, my heady chaos. So
five times a day I sat down for readings and prayers knowing
only that elsewhere others did the same. It was enough
for a while. Still a wilderness and perhaps I only found
a few crumbs and caught trout so small I had to toss them back,
but when you write of the relief a person feels when finally
turning themselves and their tasks over to a greater authority,
I remember ever so faintly the smell of yeast and how my
fingertips felt against scales, my back bent over the Psalter.

xviii.

The sky was heavy today, Thomas. By noon I'd made good
headway in tearing myself apart so I walked the circumference
of the city with my own bones tossed in a sack over my shoulder.
I clutched this thing that chafes as if it were my penance instead
of my doing. Twice I called out, so God sent five thousand blackbirds
to throng about me. Everything was shredded and carried piecemeal
into alfalfa fields. For a brief moment I was *carrion* instead of *carrying*.
Then a thought, or a dog, careened through the pasture startling
everything. The birds took to the tops of the cottonwoods as if each
pair of black wings was both an elegy to gold and a prelude to green,
the clouds nothing but foreshadowing. Later my own voice came to me,
saying, *Pull yourself together*. So I did, bone by bone, and came home
knowing only that here in this body, as in the world, the seasons
are ever changing. Today, the sky was heavy, Thomas.

XIX.

When I placed a stone on my tongue, a friend told me
not to be too hard on myself, as if the stone were in my hand
and I was using it to bash my head. But my mouth is not gored,
wind and sand have worn the stone's edges smooth, so I did not
try to explain, and the rock in my mouth didn't even whimper.
I have been talking for decades now, and maybe my voice
is nothing in the sea of words, just one more small abrasion
but my friend's ears must be ringing and what have I said?
If silence is more awkward than speech, it is because finally
we feel the weight that is always on our tongues. So I am
a slow learner and need a reminder to become quiet and
even then, my thoughts run like a deep spring. If I cannot go
into the desert to become a hermit, I will take the desert
into my mouth and begin to practice with friends.

XX.

Right now I am in rapture. Winter has a way of putting us
in our places and mine seems to be here at the kitchen table
with a pen and stationery. Outside the streets are empty and
snow falls uninterrupted. I might be a solitary witness to how
all humanity has been plucked from their daily busyness and
carried off to the heavens, but more likely the whole world's
just gone home. Either way, I can hardly grieve. Truth is, Thomas,
I am too cold and starved for solitude to miss anyone. Besides,
I expected this, and not because of all the doomsday predictions
or because I think one day Armageddon will be more than a hill
tourists climb, but rather because this happens every year. As if
by some great design, the end of fall brings the blueprints for loss
to the table. We may crinkle our faces, but when the storms set in,
we all head home to begin dealing with the disappeared.

XXI.

Every day I walk by the ditch. It's a real ditch and a metaphor.
The fields get irrigated and I get reminded of where I come from
and where I could go back to. Falling's easy. Sometimes I slip up
and enjoy myself. There's no fault in that. Gravity's at work even
when I don't think about it, so I keep my feet on the path and let
the sky be the sky, the ditch remain something for farmers. Trust
is no easy task. Each hour is the accumulation of spent minutes and
the path under my feet is simply dirt. By the time I get home, more
paint has peeled from my trailer and hard as I try not to, I expect
something, a revelation, or at least a proverb, to be unveiled, but
from what I get to see, there's no writing under the paint, just metal.
At least what's been exposed shines. Life has its bare spots,
even when you live in a trailer that is a little more than a shell.
If you put your ear to this one, you'd hear the ocean or weeping.

XXII.

I invited you for rice and asparagus but you stood me up.
I can't blame you. Here I am learning to walk a whole new line
of thought, and at the same time, a fallen woman, hoping
to make amends. Some days it seems neither my doings nor
my undoings measure up. When you didn't show, I sat down,
sighing, with your books. Once, a teacher pulled me from the
classroom to bandage my knees before going back to the lecture.
It was fortunate I tripped. A little salve goes a long way and
how often do we get the luxury of wounds that make sense, visible
ones that show the world our place and need? Compassion is vital.
You, Thomas, have never seen me or witnessed the ways I am torn.
Nonetheless, it is as if you thrust your pen into doubt and came out
writing for every reader. When I finish your books, then, I will
mourn your death and celebrate your presence at my table.

XXiii.

When I moved out, I inherited the family Bible. I've had it years
now and you'd think I'd know what to expect in those pages,
but I've just realized that what's underlined is my childhood.
Anyone can see our entire household by where my mother's pen
set down. It is a whole new text uncovered. Every single parable
on drink has a star next to it, both the drinks that lead to downfall
and the drinks given to the dying so they might forget. Passages
on disciplining your children are marked with a hard line and next
to every good wife in Proverbs is the word (busy) in parenthesis.
A few sections are noted tentatively, in pencil, as if adultery was a
suspicion instead of a certainty, and in Philippians, the single word
imprisonment is underlined and later, the part that tells you to do
all things without grumbling. *Do all things without grumbling* hits
hard. At fifteen, I thought my mother was just in denial and said so.

XXIV.

I have lived half my life in the desert. My spine is bleached
and my hide tanned. I'm beaten and thirsty, but not for years
have I wanted to live anywhere else. I'd rather face the fence
each morning and see what the wind stuck in it. There is always
temptation and a quick look at litter, or the city, illuminates a lot.
In fact, there's so much light you have to leave town to redeem
the sky. Redemption is important. I look for signs. Stellar jays
in the mountains. Pheasants in the valley. The ones on posts
by the roadside that say *leaving city limits*. I am a weak woman
and don't want to make my own erosion easy, so I live in this harsh
climate and try to stay at least a stone's throw from the big flubbery.
For years I was separated from the city by a small canyon. Now it's an
even more slender buffer, a quick field and a low river. Every day
I grasp at sand and try to keep the topsoil from blowing off.

XXV.

At the laundromat, I remember humility. This load's not even
mine, it's my grandmother's but here, applying spot remover,
there is no differentiation. We are all stained. Machines
thrum and the news is on tv in the background. It's almost
peaceful, the way clothes go round and round and the woman
articulating obscenities to her sister keeps them almost
under her breath. I have put so many quarters into the slots
and yet each time I have the same expectation: water will run,
my clothes will be washed clean, and for one folded moment
I can forget the inevitability of dirt and sweat. Almost.
The public spectacle of the laundromat serves many purposes,
and if it's reserved for the poor, no one doubts what happens to
the clothes of the rich. Eventually, we all have to own up.
Each item that frays in the spin cycle unravels a common thread.

XXVİ.

I am not as messed up as I think, nor am I any less flawed than
I suspect. Human, I am therefore liable to foible my life away.
I deserve simultaneous kudos and beratings. It's a double bind.
More like a double blind psych experiment. Usually doctor and
patient are two different people. My way simplifies things.
I am the only person who doesn't know if what I administer
to myself is placebo or the real stuff. I'm not talking about drugs.
I'm talking about everything. Sleep diet denomination light
barometric pressure genetics longitude *et al.* The results indicate
only that something's working while something else isn't. Sugar
pills can cause side effects. If I give myself too much latitude,
who knows what'll go askew and what'll mend. To understand
the impact of all the variables would take a god. To accept
that everything is variable may perhaps be a task I'm up to.

XXVii.

Down at the adobe pit off Edith, the old anglo has forgotten
the English word for bucket. He came up with several variations
in Spanish as well as a number of hand gestures. I got the picture.
The *bote* holds the foul slop that will waterproof the mud and
every language has its holes. A different man might show me how
to trowel crosswise so the rains would run a slower course but
this one helped me envision a communication that can't be contained.
Maybe English is his second language, but I would prefer to believe
that it's his first and he's simply outgrowing it, that a new universe
and all the necessary expressions can be created anywhere there is
dirt. God, how I'd love to grow a new tongue or at least put this one
to better use. If an old man's mouth can change, then there's hope
for us all. Perhaps our ever flapping lips can form all the *pidgins*
it's going to take to cover with wings this muddied cathedral.

XXViii.

I am all wound up. If you give a good tug on the end of the line
I could spin across the kitchen floor for hours, maybe even weeks.
There are days, when like a spent top, I simply fall to the floor
and collapse. No longer at the liberty of the string, all those
dizzying whims, I rest. And with my face pressed to linoleum,
my vision is clear. (Look, the corner of a tile is coming loose.)
Despair doesn't blink. There is a place beyond wincing where
the world seems to hold entirely different possibilities, distinct
from what someone else thinks my good life will be, distinct from
from what I'd hoped. All my expectations are laid across my knee
and broken by an invisible hand. And here, I find this new source
of compassion, the biggest compassion, that smashes all the crockery
except for one cup and one plate. With wonder, I realize this
is all I need. (Look, another corner of my hubris has come loose.)

XXIX.

A ring-necked pheasant scuttles into brush and my vision wanders
on up the mountain. Perspective is shifty as a coyote. Last night
outside my window I heard what I thought was humming, a hum
that rose into a frenzy of yip and howl. So I mistook a pack of beasts
for a few men. I should have joined in, my mind was chasing geese
and making rabble. And now standing in this fallow field, I am torn
between the rise of rock and the lay of pasture. Strewn feathers
and remnants of breast bones are signs to keep heart and lay low.
If I have written myself onto brittle ground, it is because I want to
crack something. Let my feet break the old cut stalks, my steps soften
the frozen soil. Let me trip up in the furrows from the first plowing
so that one day, soon, I'll be ready when the alfalfa rises up, green
proletariat, and carries me up slope and steep, to that high place,
where my teeth will bleat like old sheep, *I saw the rocks coming.*

XXX.

It's the middle of the night, the sky is all creased and no wind
moves anything. My head, stuck out the front door, is as still and
as clouded. A cranium makes a decent observatory, but my eyes
are common pupils, yawning at the blackboard above me, as if
it's been erased, as if I don't know what to look for. In the recesses
of my mind, I can still make out a few bright spots and try to find
ways to form constellations but everything seems like an imposition.
My day was no better. I took up with crows, a long list of gripes
and an endless procession of *cause and effect*. The sun will shine
on the barest branch. It gets to me. So I balled up sleep and tucked
it into an armchair, thinking I could salvage something or at least
lessen my resistance. Soon the earth will have spun round again
the oldest story, a new day, and perhaps tired and played out,
I'll be able to accept this and all the other mournings.

XXXI.

Last week I had an intuition that someone I knew might
be affected by a story I saw on the news of a plane crash
simply because it fell in an ocean near friends. A flicker
of a thought, I quickly discarded it as I do every day
I hear of car wrecks on the other side of town. Nonetheless
I wrote a few letters and thought about how impossible
it is to mourn for this planet, to even fathom the simplest
bombing, to adequately cherish anyone, to expect to go
unscathed. Tonight a friend I hadn't really expected called
with grief bolted to her heart. She'd received my letter (I
hadn't mentioned my concern) and lost six friends. I could
say little. Death makes sense to me, in its inevitability,
life should have limits, but I still stagger in each context,
crash or cancer or shock, stagger for those of us left behind.

XXXII.

One of my friends has a small farm. The first time I dropped by,
her kids, thriving as weeds, gave me the full tour, rattling off
the names of every flower and plant in the ground. I met goats
and chickens and got the family history and temperament of each
animal. Later, my friend bent down, sorted through some foliage,
and pulled. Then she took my hands and placed a daikon root
in them. No one's ever done that before. I blushed. All night
I dreamt of sweet peas and bok choy, a flourishing plot, as if
my friend had also cultivated the bed I sleep in. It was akin to
enlightenment, a touch, only in this case everything turned green.
In the morning, I picked up a shovel. This part, where you learn
to dig, is not easy. The sun beats down on your back for days and
water, well, the soil's thirst is consuming. You begin to hunger
for harvests. You begin to search for what's sustainable.

XXXIII.

A decade ago I tried to sell vacuum cleaners door to door.
It didn't last. The boss wore so much gold, he was one big
glint. The training went something like sparkle-sparkle-dirty-
dirty-whir-wallet-whir-clean-gleam. I was floored. On a break,
a co-worker told me she'd had her first kid at sixteen and lost
her front tooth to a boyfriend's fist, so now her mother babysits
while she works and really she just wants to get by, *No quiero
mucho*. Then she pulled up her shirt to show me stretchmarks
as if they were caused by generalized desire. The phrase, *I don't
want much*, was to become the credo I live by in the face of lost
jobs and poor wages. More than that, it's how I'd like to live,
simply, wanting little. Time whittles desire down to the barest
essentials. Soon enough we'll all be dust and meanwhile
our lives remain so dirty, I doubt anything can clean us up.

XXXIV.

I got a splinter imbedded in my thumb when I was working
on the back fence. An accident, I never meant to force a piece
of this big world into my flesh. A more receptive person
might leave splinters in and have faith in white blood cells,
but I am sitting here with a needle poised over a flame.
Anyone who has ever seen a simple plank warp or twist
with the pull of the grain will remember wood is alive,
even after cut. So I am afraid. It is a question of intimacy.
If this small sliver of wood gets into my blood it could travel
to my heart. In the course of a year many slivers might
accumulate there. They might happen to form a lean-to,
a shack or little shanty, and suddenly, I would find myself
unexpectedly wedged open, a wide and welcoming thing.
Most days though, I am only so many timid molecules.

XXXV.

Yesterday the sky filled with petroleum. On the ground,
not a bush, but a packing plant burned. Perhaps someone finally
decided to ship the family business into the atmosphere, to expose
smoke and mirrors, debt and billow. Even onlookers were consumed
by the idea of stuff and stuffing. No one was evacuated. I was
disappointed but the wind was fierce. We stayed in our boxes
with the windows shut against anything gone adrift while the wind
worked away at the smoke and took that roiling to a better place
than this city, perhaps over the volcanoes and onto mesas, maybe
twisting towards the Sangre de Cristos. I don't know where it went.
It must have dissipated and spread out like the lineage of nuclear
families, searching for better work and better spouses. I stayed home.
Toxins travel more than I do. Even cyanide spilled into a river
has a better chance of seeing the world, of catching fish.

XXXVİ.

Here is sweetness: I can't lick my fingers clean this dusk.
I am a marked woman, stained scarlet, though I've come home
alone as ever. A friend made me notice the mulberry tree and
the young man, who, with mouth open and hands upstretched,
looked like Everylover. So I walked to the tree and was seduced
by all those bent branches. Still on the tip of my tongue from
small talk was my heritage, everything unspoken or forgotten,
but I picked berries. The Lover told how the Choctaw sent
300 dollars to the Irish during the Potato Famine while I ate
berries. Everywhere is generosity and despair. I can't even see
all the branches. The berries I left for the birds might not be any
sweeter than the ones I ate, but I regret I couldn't climb higher.
And driving home I actually wanted to be pulled over by cops,
or William Carlos Williams, so I could be seen for who I am.

XXXVII.

Somewhere in the community a person is belligerent, defensive,

wielding a frying pan or a vase with yesterday's wildflowers.

Here is only the symbol. A tail fanned and dark against the sky.

Even the light is tentative as if a quick fight could change everything.

My own body is still between worlds, waking slowing, rasped upon.

I got here by grackle, to this place with my face pressed to a broken

window, so I have choices to make more than simply whether

I return to sleep or brew coffee. What's broken shouldn't always be

ignored but this cracking parts the tin hull of the trailer so birdcalls

can flap straight to my ears to herald choices, to herald questions.

It is so early a few people must still be up from last night, early enough

clouds hang over the valley as if the sun won't soon burn them up.

I could be lonely. I could be happy I'm not arguing with another person.

I could be sun and shadow, a repetitive scratch, a few sound waves.

XXXVIII.

My dog always finds bones in the alfalfa field. I am used
to these small sunbleached reminders of death, but yesterday,
when I pried her mouth open, all I could see was teeth. She'd found
a calf's jaw, and despite my objections, kept turning it over, as if
her own teeth and the ones on this other jaw should come together
and engage in the chewing of cud. The sound of teeth worked over
by teeth is not unfamiliar. I come from a long line of cogs,
generations of gears locked in the motion of large machines:
gods and countries, marriages and booze, recessions or community
codas. Once in the Dakotas my kin got massacred in a sod house
and their blood turned a rope into a lynch mob. Not even this planet
can cease spinning. If I am less useful than my lineage, perhaps
I've been cranked less, but my own mouth is still full of teeth,
my body one big bitemark, my life perpetually grinding.

XXXIX.

I spent the morning mythed. I pushed a truck up a gravel drive
and after it rolled down, I pushed it up towards the field again.
In the cab, a friend popped the clutch, repeatedly. As if we were
at a cineplex that only featured flicks about feet and women's
hands on tailgates, finally I'd had enough. And yet, I kept at it.
I am nothing especially sinewed and like any vehicle I have limits,
but I wanted to show some gratitude. Earlier in the day, he'd
had the foresight to haul off the carcass of a turkey that got downed
by domestic dogs behind my trailer. All morning before he arrived
I'd been watching the upturned feet expecting, or hoping for, a plot
twist. Perhaps I made a silly fuss, but we all have stuff to push or
carry, and occasionally trading off seems reasonable. And so what
if some days I'd rather push a two ton truck I don't own than carry
the 25 pound carcass of a bird I heard getting its neck snapped.

XL.

I hit the road as if it were a linear place to shake my fist.
Near Wiggins, Nebraska all the truckers switched to driving
in the left lane, a game forcing me to pass on the right.
At Ovid, everything changed. It was the least flashy form
of metamorphosis, the kind where everything reverts
to what is most basic. Picture a diorama of a girl in a car
on a road, the whole scenario cut with Occam's razor.
There is no map on the dash, only a few signs by the ditch
let you know the car did not veer off at Waco, or Littleton,
or Belvue. The horizon stretches to a vanishing point where
grief must have gone, though nothing gets any closer or farther.
Only a dotted yellow line separates absurdity from my sense
that I could merge with anything trying to cross the Platte River,
the Uncompahgre, follow any river to a usable bridge.

XLİ.

Rock, burr, shard, I have stepped on many things where I saw
only dirt, then panged alert, lifted a bare sole to find blood
beading. This time softness startled me into balancing on one leg
to watch what was already red, a velvet ant, continue its solitary
journey. This preservation was so incidental, a hair's breadth
fluke, that for the first time I believed the architecture of my foot
was no accident but something predestined. Where my flesh is not
holds the same capacity for intimacy as where my flesh is. Today
the absence of my body made safe passage, an underpass for
the universe. Now even my breath is arched as if I can have faith
that at least occasionally my bones will rise and fall in ways not
unkind but rather attentive to needs other than my own, attentive
to my need to make space for the world around me, to make places
on my body receptive to the lightest touch, the smallest pleasures.

XLII.

At the start of World War II, there was no word for *bomb* in Navajo,
but considering soreness of land, the muscular grief of the bereaved,
code talkers hit upon *ache*. Half a century later, that word has dropped
from the sky and exploded in my mouth. My body *aches*. The person
who fell upon me I call *friend, beloved* but now here under covers
is Hiroshima. Or is it Nagasaki? My cells carry the imprint of where
another body was. In this glossary, my molecules are encrypted,
this old flesh turned to an older wall upon which shadows were cast
to stay past the setting of suns, past the fading of visible bruise.
Synapses don't stop firing. Perhaps in the flesh between knee and hip
of every lover there lies an Oklahoma, a North Ireland, the femur
nothing but a pipe some teen capped in his garage. We have worlds
of flesh to comprehend and with words as weapons, words as elixir,
maybe we can learn not to long for one person and bomb another.

XLiii.

Sometimes you have to clear the way for what comes next
so I am not unhappy that I know how to swing a sledgehammer.
However yesterday when every surface called out for rough contact
and my muscles were fraught with impetus to strike, I knew
all I would have made was rubble. So I sat still as a person can,
pent and undifferentiated, biding my time until sense or violence
would carry me away. When the storm hit, lightning left me
awed. I wanted to be that downpour. Or any arroyo. My tongue
less than subtly rumbling is no breaking news, but the storm was
good and wet. Nothing lasts. With the sky washed and wrung out,
even ravens know, this is an appropriate place to make waves,
to vocalize silt. I myself am still rippling, reflecting my own grin
and slapping an imaginary arthritic's tic knee, relieved, because
this time what I felt forecast in this body wasn't my responsibility.

XLIV.

I thought I could tell what's forested from what's not but sometimes
night gets pitched so thoroughly not even the boundary between
sky and land can be discerned. If my eyes adjust enough for tentative
steps, too often the only pining I recognize is still my own body.
So to walk, purposefully awkward, in the dark, is to remember
how to bump into the less seen. I learned the contour of one lake
by mapping reflected constellations while descending through thickets.
I reached the beach aware of my shins, my blood, that I walked alone.
Or almost. It was a manmade lake. A shirker's style of clear cut. Stumps
had been watered until roots gave way, let go and rose up, rolling
over on what had gone down. I grieved with those ghosts, rocking
through time into a sleep cradled by a bent seedling and a thornbush.
As long as what's original, or ravaged, remains even half-submerged,
I want to be the kind of magpie that dives beyond what glints.

XLV.

I wake and find the sky opaque, frozen tactile. I am neither
more nor less fond than I was yesterday, yet everything missed
has made the air solid in its emptiness. If my desire is particular,
the result is not. Now that I can't see what's deciduous, I could long
for the ditchbank, cellophane off a pack of cigarettes, a fence post
or stranger. I would like to pull a knife from the kitchen drawer, walk
outside and begin paring the space between things down to a more
palatable size. Separation irks, makes me a window. I am saddened
capable—not everything should be split apart—but as leaves go
falling, I don't try to put them back on branches. I could. So *there*,
there is space between the atomic particles of anything solid. What
comes between you and I, comes between everything. Cold expands
me until time is a bird wing, distance only a flap. Exposed, pipes
freeze. Unfold my insular view and I warm to receive the unbidden.

XLVİ.

My lips are raw, having made some pilgrimage across a pasture
of now bent ears. When dawn cracked, I quit thrashing and baled
outside. I would still cut my tongue with my own teeth if I could
temper my past, soften the blow of letting another person know me.
But history repeats itself, or I repeat it, yammering. My own words
yip and bay, beckon and go nipping at unhealed parts until I am
half-driven, half-chaste into alfalfa. If the sky mirrors my torpid
circling, the way geese wing it, the far end of the field seems sensible
as a destination. I stand unconvinced of the merits of magnetism but
at first rustle, geese startle and I can't prevent myself from turning
as an old cowboy emerges from brush. Wielding a lasso, he looks
long over me, then brimmed, turns to survey more frozen landscape.
I am no cow straying, though one day wild-trampling, the next
unmoving. *Come on*, I cajole, *Corral me. Loosen these latches.*

XLVii.

Here I admit lapse. Thomas, I have called too many valleys
concave. For months I stood in the shadow of clouds, blank-
faced, soothsaying. Moment by moment, my world dropped off
until the horizon became an abstraction edged with birds. Vision
fractured with my grandmother's spine: I would catch geese flying
south, others north, sun then shadow, ultraviolet light then x-rays.
The arcs were too big for me to comprehend, so small-minded
I slipped through the cracks of interpretation. When you lose
track of which migration is happening, this is a good time to study
magyarul. Understand: seasons kept turning but I stood stuck
in the gray area before loss while grandma struggled in room 406.
So I threw a tether to another grammar and asked to be consumed
because I wanted to be justifiably vexed. Hope sometimes needs
more than what we already know and *előadásmód* is perception.

XLViii.

Perhaps I do miss church. My rooster has taken to crowing
call and response with birds downfield which means mornings
I think of Matthew and Mark and the phrase *wherever three*
or more are gathered and then wonder if everyone living off
Guadalupe Trail is knit together by common livestock. Maybe
distance between houses shrinks with the carrying of soundwaves,
scattering of corn, fetching of eggs. Certainly I like my bird's part
and derive some pre-dawn solace in my awareness of other bird-
owners. Often I get cooped up enough to wish I could throw
my voice or a stone across the big ditch and see where it lands
instead of just tossing off letters. If I long for some response
that decries alienation, still I stalk the field, unable or unwilling
to be more forthright about my interactions. Three crows land
on fenceposts and I have to admit: *I like this communal solitude.*

XLİX.

I have a garden Thomas. Last year at this time I had food
stamps. It was a hard call to make this season. I wasn't sure
I could afford to invest the hours and hours working dirt
instead of searching for scrap work. Manure reminds me
of a craps shoot. Despite selecting seeds, I hardly know
what kind of fruits and vegetables my labor will bare, if
the plants will thrive or find the soil deplete, my attentions
somehow lacking. And I still have no goat or cow, no field
of wheat and my own mill, so my efforts only supplement
a diet meager as my pocketbook and cooking ability. But
already I am eating it up. Seeds sprouted. If some withered,
many didn't. All round I see green and within that, ladybugs
and butterflies. I can kneel and smell basil or lemon balm,
mint and oregano. I see tiny peppers still housed in buds.

L.

Before I began this letter, I sat with a pen and pad and practiced
writing two lines, *heng* and *shu*. Solitary pen strokes. I copied them
over until the ink ran like water. A fish can also be drawn with two
lines. As a child I'd draw half, my church leader finishing it off, but
I have to tell you Merton, that particular two-line symbol, scratched
in dirt with a shared stick, was nothing familiar to rivers. If the line
I drew was an open bowl, empty, expectant, the line that came down
was hard, clasped like a vice. Picture half-circles hinged and pivoting
on fear. The space inside the thinking was so small I could hardly
breathe. Part of me is still curled up trembling. I've taken two decades
to return with questions, so please be patient. I still balk at brimstone
lingo, but I would like, and need, to write to you, open and inept,
as a child should be allowed to be when first shaping the letter *a*—
because here, in this dialogue, I am a child and make small streams.

LI.

What comes to mind here is the word *hogwash*, as if you
were still saying it, reminding me if a monk can say *hogwash*,
inversely an anti-zealot can speak the word *God*. Personally
I suspect God would see everything in the spectrum as valuable.
(Perhaps a baboon's ass is in some way red as a lotus.) I hope so.
Any fall from grace might easily spur an addiction to ladders but
this perpetual desire to *rung up* each other creates a sad wheel
that leaves us all both trod upon and trodding. I don't know how
to dismantle hierarchies. Looking up or looking down only makes
things better and worse off. I can't be optimistic. Recently crying,
a tear dropped onto my glasses. That displaced bead, suspended
in time and space, startled me. I realized my head was bowed,
a body of old prayer. My sadness lifted with this recognition
of another lens through which the world is clarified, distorted.

LII.

I keep dropping things, a pen to the floor, my morning coffee
tipped spilling on my desk, a plate shattered, keys misplaced
on the gravel drive, mail disappearing forever into some slot.
Maybe I've become accident-prone but letting go is complicated
and all these little mishaps feel like practice for something bigger
as if my thumb and forefingers oppose my grandma's impending
parting, grasp at her by releasing everything trivial. Make believe
explanations almost make it better, almost soothe this future loss.
To feel sad already makes me feel clumsy, jumping the gun to get to
my abandonment. Sure she's 91, but still bright, resilient, hasn't had
the flu since World War II. Nonetheless these days she hears songs
from the first war, slips back past my grandfather to her childhood.
My gut tells me that she's leaving me, letting me glimpse the old ones
she'll join, singing *there'll be moonlight and roses when I return.*

LIII.

What Mary told the breadtruck driver in Iowa gives great heart.
When he asked *Why me?* she said, *Because you are the least*
apt instrument I could find, and therefore people will know that
these are my words and not yours. If ineptitude lends credibility,
it puts a chink in assumptions. The extraordinary will manifest
in the ordinary—which means nothing can be taken for granted
or glossed over—less direct vehicles of God could be anywhere. Plus,
I find strange solace picturing the man back when he was just driving
his truck and yet the *most-racked* person in the vicinity. Am I
irreverent, to think the upper structure might enjoy (and employ)
the lucidity of dream states where one thing plays off another and
even language is another opportunity? I mean he delivered bread,
the earthly kind, and he got the spiritual, a vision, and he spoke
delivering it to the rest of us through time. What a happy thing.

LIV.

Between my body and the green mountain, a barbed wire fence.
This side is dust, a few sparse sunbaked weeds, a wooden pallet
I have chosen to rest upon. Today the wire, which easily could
be pulled apart or rolled under, creates an effective segregation.
I wouldn't even call what I feel, looking towards that lush place,
longing, more like some strange acceptance of things happening
in time. I am reminded how I stopped reading St. John of the Cross
when he referenced being weaned from the tit of God. I simply closed
the book for the night, not sad, having recognized my desolation
within a larger context. I want to lead more than a coddled life so
I will accept less, even much less when necessary. Sitting in dust,
feeling thirst and dryness, close but still separated from what's
wild springing, I know my brittle. Today this fenceline in Colorado
is where I need to be aware. I don't need to understand why.

LV.

The river that welcomed itself over my grandmother's stoop and
lifted her piano from the floor as if it were some child's toy designed
to float downstream, scurried like its namesake, got into everything.
After the rains came a time of shoveling mud and wood warping.
The river my uncle stopped was named after a fruit, something
sweet like a cherry or apricot. Picture white caps as abundant as
blossoms. It seemed biblical in proportion, his retelling of the parting
of the waters, though literally the mechanism of some simple dam
(plus someone's political discretion) slowed that river so my cousin
could be found and pulled from under the boulder where his body
had been swept after the rafting accident. Every family lives with
water or lack of water as myth. Perhaps sorrow always gets wedged
under something and solace at times is no more than a chance to stay
this long river, briefly, to air what's waterlogged, and grieve a bit.

LVİ.

The hens like it when I stay up until dawn. Such basic creatures,
all time not resting is the desire to eat, take a dirt bath. Only when
I don't sleep do they lay claim to a farmer's daughter, usually I'm
on some odd swing shift. These days my need for mourning
is pronounced, so at dawn I watch the dark turn over to light,
and at dusk, the light to dark, such tenuous shifts from one clarity
to another. The alfalfa was cut and baled right before I went north
to bury my grandmother but shot back up so fast the funeral
seemed a season in and of itself. To walk a furrowed field makes
rejuvenation seem possible so I gather greens for the birds, maybe
just for the gathering. This state, where I'm so long awake, is less
medicated, so likely I'm a little more fragile, but morning glories
open, I hear woodpeckers and startle pheasants into low flight.
A person needs smallness, to sit and listen to water run the ditch.

LVii.

Saint John of the Cross came after me in a pick-up and hit hard.
Granted, as friends keep reminding me, there was another person
involved, a regular middleaged swigger, trying to reach a friend
by following an afternoon drunk down Broadway. Ten beers, more
bars, that's par. I can't write his story even if I wanted to. But mine?
Red wine sanctified gets swallowed as the blood of Christ, so maybe
Saint John of the Cross came in the form of a draft, drunk or whispered.
I can hear him saying, *Strike her Phillip. Hit her at dusk. Let her live*
to know how little of the soul's dark night she's experienced. Remind
her of the journey ahead. But Thomas, I'm no novice, was already poor,
with enough near death experiences to rename the days of the week, so
I'm confused. After the crash I stood in the gutter, shaking and shaking
peoples hands, asking and forgetting names over and over, my gratitude
overwhelming. Now I fear what will happen if I can't interpret this sign.

LViii.

One of the last things my grandmother and I shared
was coincidental interest in the Braille alphabet. I had been
studying it because I was frustrated with a sighted friend who
I considered unable to *see* and so I wrote him letters in ink
dot Braille. She began the alphabet at 90, her own sight neither
great nor gone. Maybe her interest sparked after talking with
a neighbor who was blind. I'd witnessed that interaction between
errands, noting only how sociable my gramma had become lately.
Everyone was *sweetie* or *honey* and not simply because
names were forgotten but because compassion and tolerance
had lodged in her skeleton. I picture her bones as cathedrals.
When I found her Braille card, we talked and I ran my fingers
over the bumps, realizing I'd both misinterpreted the charts
I'd been studying and forgotten about literal blindness.

LIX.

I hope for no electrical fire in this old trailer. I don't intend
to covet the things I've accumulated here, but still in honesty,
I'd prefer no fire. If there must be flames, then my prayer would
be for the burning to come on a day I'm here or have at least
remembered to leave the window open so my cats can escape.
Is even that desire too much? This time of dismantling seems
gradually thorough and too appropriate, but as usual I long for
control and wish for that option some of time. Today, I can say,
with albeit scrutable certainty, that I won't continue indefinitely
to neglect the giving away of excess. I hardly think I can afford
to. Figuring out what's excess is the greater task. Thomas, know:
I prepare with joy and trepidation. If my fingers remain mittened
by foibles and my knuckles are only beads on an abacus holding
creaking count of my flaws, my hands are at last unpocketed.

LX.

In the crash, my windshield miraculously only sustained cracks.
My bones feel equally riddled with hairlines. Illusions, however,
at least some of my rickety crutches, shattered, lie broken and
splintered all over the roadway. I recognize the pieces for what
they always were, scraps of ideologies, a few scavenged rivets,
grooves I'd worn soft with the set of my mind. Today's misaligned
posture, my changed and awkward carriage, is the same skeleton
I've always had, simply exposed, broke of old muscle and ligature
habit, cold turkey, as if reborn or maybe re-membered. Mortality
is nothing new. *Deja vu*. I knew all this fear but kept a sustaining
ignorance or forgetfulness. So my mind is divided between grief
and gratitude. I live in two hemispheres and the bridge seems icy.
Not in reality slippery, I nonetheless slide from side to side, erratic
as the other driver who crossed a yellow couplet twice that night.

LXI.

I am not unfamiliar with this state. Almost 20 years of living
in this city, and still September 11th, I thought I was overseas.
Raised on airbases, anti-American sentiment was daily bread,
bomb threats mundane, grief and guilt for trespassing enormous.
The familiarity is dismal and foreboding. Black Forest or desert,
fear stinks on any terrain and creates a prescription for paranoia.
Back in 5th grade I was accused of aiding anti-American terrorists
in Germany. I'd taped over a lock so us kids could escape the cold
after recess but military police wielding guns caught us. I worry.
Paranoia misplaces everything and as Thanksgiving approaches
(like a side of succotash next to more pressing preoccupations)
I can't help but wonder if the executive pardon will fall yet again
on a domesticated turkey while past scapegoats stay penned up
and more get made. It's predictable as violets begetting violets.

LXII.

With every fall comes flapping. Birds migrate and now flags—
a whole gaggle—beat in the wind, slapped up quickly as if
subconsciously we think the *united* that we stick with *states*
is something we can wing. But hollow words and a predilection
to tar and feather don't constitute a bird, so I can't find the flags
particularly reassuring and the ones on the road confound me.
All vehicles potentially threaten more than air quality, and after
my head-on with a drunk driver, I find the association disturbing.
Who knows, perhaps the flags are like daytime running lights,
help get attention, I certainly see them coming, but tend now
to think of blind spots and wonder what view is being obscured
by this patriotism, figure fatalities involving literal American flags
are on the rise even if the driving is the same as always. Meanwhile
cranes coo over this city as if we were infants asleep in a cradle.

LXiii.

In the hospital everyone's patient with the shocked, a certain loss
of memory predicted by doctors so forgetfulness is forgiven, almost
overlooked. The mental ward's inherently repetitive, our movements
dictated by clocks advertising antidepressants, a Pavlovian strategy
that associates any hope of food or smokes or visits, any literal
or metaphorical *looking up*, with drugs— or the tv, which was also
elevated, and fairly pacifying, until the bombing of Afghanistan.
Then my mouth exploded—or began to. Seized by a look from staff,
I bit my tongue. If I wanted to be able to remember, I couldn't forget
who has the power to define *compliance*. Now that I'm back out,
I've reverted to counting votes for my insomnia, and I'm happy
that I can say anything I want, and for now at least, only phones
and not my head can be wiretapped. But I still scour people's faces
for side effects of shock treatment and listen for what's forgotten.

LXIV.

I am neither that far off the tracks nor am I particularly close

to any of those lines that lead deft and certain to wherever

they lead. From the trailer I picture empirical ladders, flattened

out, rung by rung, getting to some place logical, making progress.

This structure is so thin, so earth-perched and tenuous, I actually

feel trains approaching in the night. In the past I'd get wistful as if

I also could engineer a little surety or simply dream a bit. Both

my body and imagination have stretched out on those journeys,

but I lose weight, unable to stomach much, while trains get heavier,

laden with the stuffs of war. Consequently, my desire to hop one

of those trains has flagged. Heavy metals weigh on the present,

leave me lead-brained. What was once a tremor is now a shudder.

Nightly I mourn the departure of small solace. Even my response

to the whistles is delayed so what I hear is past tense: *blown.*

LXV.

I sit anchored on my stoop bereft of all things glimmering,
as if hope has blown a fuse, knocking out even the stars.
The emptiness is deceptive. Whatever's up in our atmosphere
always diminishes any steady shine to a flicker and tonight
that intermittent muting is simply not so intermittent. Nothing
is visible in this blankety blank sky so I can't pretend to navigate
with any clear sense of bearings. The dead keep getting buried
under rubble and smoke rises round the globe. I can't pretend
I'm not saddened or that I know what to make of life. Earlier
the moon rose briefly into a clearing to expose the dark night
as cloud-crammed, and was gone. Perhaps the first job of light
is to illuminate what's doing the obscuring. The visual silence
has become almost consolation, a mother's counsel, *Hush child,*
maybe today you can be disillusioned by what you've seen.

LXVI.

The sky is back, looking all starry-eyed. I found it in the desert,
between gas pipes and gypsum mines. After all the jets setting
down on buildings, over forty days and forty nights of *carpet die*m
bombings, after my own moods have ricocheted around my body
splintering my thoughts into shrapnel that flies from my mouth
and lodges in the ears of friends and innocent bystanders, I needed
to hightail it out of town, take refuge where the wind could have at
my anger and I could look up without grief over what falls. Shooting
stars were a welcome prediction. It's easy to forget people count
these things, hard for me to remember the cyclic nature of everything
though I'm bipolar as the world. So I went to the desert at midnight
and sat there with my neck bent back like scrub grass under the wind
and I watched the Leonid meteor shower as if I could learn to love
what's ungraspable and fleeting, what crosses my peripheral vision.

LXVii.

This year I made many mistakes that blossomed in the night-
shade family. If I had a tenuous faith when I began gardening,
I let what happened on asphalt pave it over. All I could see
when I looked at the plants was my inability to eat solid food.
The idea of weeding hurt. The whole plot was a reminder of loss
and I didn't want that to flourish, so I quit watering, as if letting
the garden die would ease my awareness of changes in my body.
When I began to heal, I was forced to look at all I'd given up on.
Amid the tangled wreck of the overripe or stunted, I found eight
foot tomato plants. Monstrosities. I felt relieved my Frankensteins
were fruit-bearing, that I hadn't neglected anything more ominous.
The will to live is dogged. My doubt shames me and then my shame
shames me. I cultivated that a while, then got plucking. Undeserved
fruit tastes strangely. My full mouth surrenders to the bittersweet.

LXVIII.

I spent the morning casing the mesa for shells. I was struck
by the plastics that litter the dirt where people stopped to drink
and shoot a few rounds, so I picked up shotgun shells. I figured
someone ought to. Besides, this is one way to gauge a good time,
if not mine. Back in town, people attend classes so they can hide
guns officially. The course got reported on TV but war legislates
images. Although the curriculum includes strategies on avoiding
actually firing the guns, that newsreel got sawed off. What wasn't
concealed was fanaticism: the generic black silhouettes for targets
were fleshed out with Osama bin Laden's face. Mesa philosophies
seem more sensible. People simply aim at fenceposts, signs or junk,
shoot symbols of division, blow holes in the concept of ownership.
Plus the red and green shells are awful timely and trigger happy
holiday spirit. I rinse the sand off and construct bright wreaths.

LXIX.

Money's tight as a bone girdle. The constriction eases a bit
as I give what I've stashed away. This is not my usual manic
where I'll hand my last fifty cash to the first person to follow
me in a parking lot, rather more systematic, almost thoughtful.
Still, it's a meager abstraction of good will, to bundle and drop
stuff off, indiscriminately, without attention to dissemination,
awareness of actual need, or any empathy with the person
whose hands might pick it up. If I put flag stickers on the bags
someone might think I'm motivated by the times, hard-earned
global compassion, but I'm not. The less I own, the more I feel
compelled to own up to even this way of being self-centered.
I'm not thinking about refugees or the homeless, or who's more
or less poor than I am or why. I just assess what's in my closet
for what I do or don't need. One skeleton per body is plenty.

LXX.

By the time I woke up and got out of bed, night blanketed
everything. Disoriented, I wandered from window to window
until a strong sense of loss tethered me to my desk. This yank
on my heart, this small regret, sun versus no-sun, aches. Lately
daylight pummels the question, *This is it?* So I didn't expect
to feel sad not to be able to see neglected weeds, the forgotten
tools I gave up to rust. The lure of untrafficked, unringing hours
after the blue glows of neighboring tvs die, has driven me to love
night to excess. Still last week I asked my healer about the clock
in my brain. He said, *You are just contrary.* And I am, suspect
I always will be some fierce animal condemned to rise and haunt
the shadows, but if I could crawl inside this sharp pang, and stay
here, tender and sore, perhaps I could live, wanting to, knowing
night is only precious in the context of all the daily hoo-hah.

LXXI.

The pregnant co-worker of the daughter of a friend of mine was beaten
to death by her husband in Cincinnati. He hit a homerun. When she
didn't show up for her hospital shift in the morning, planes crashed
into the twin towers. $1 + 1 = 911$. Now seven more war journalists
are dead. All numbers can't B-52 correlated with some atrocity. Six
is how many cell divisions the first human clone made before giving up
that ghost. Five kids tried to walk to school in Palestine. Four what?
Inhaled anthrax. The world's mean, Thomas. Little corpses, big corpses.
Some get marked graves, others buried alive. 250,000 die daily.
More get born. Into what? Super Bowls, Super Tuesday, Black Tuesday,
everyday black markets plus economic sanctioning of *us* against
them. (Uprising kills 76.) We all live at ground zero (*zero tolerance*).
Even cows are mad in England, vets pissed off in America. Sadness
is systemic (BC, AD, PTSD). There's nothing new on the grapevine.

LXXII.

Lately I've felt spurned and sore, found myself wanting the world
to woo me back from the brink, this icy lip of sadness. Story-book
solutions don't impress me and I try not to shirk from responsibility
so when I found myself in a canoe on a lake in midwinter, I turned
to my friend and said, pointing to a shaded canyon, *Let's go there.*
So we did. We rowed out of the sun and towards backwater edged
in by rock cliff. Paddling in the middle of an empty unwinded lake,
time takes its time. We progressed despite my *ohs,* the sucking sound
of the water around my oar, a pair of bald eagles, swirling patterns.
As we moved into darkness I saw a frothy section, ducks all aclack.
The wide canyon, my thin t-shirt, plus the usual brightness left me
in denial. I knew but wouldn't admit ice until we struck it, canoe
and my body riding right up onto it. When we pushed off the big
flat berg, set adrift, I could hear it, all around me, the cracking up.

LXXIII.

I found a tin can walking the drained ditch, carried it along
with me like a beggar. I got puddles, a half-buried tractor tire,
a small and sandlocked crawdad. And then in the cottonwoods
crows, calling me on everything I know and despair of in my being,
flaws, flaws, flaws. I stooped for a stone, then straightened up,
spared the birds. Although the branches were bare, I couldn't see
purpose in driving those soothsayers from one perch to the next.
Rather I thought it would be well to learn to call them by name,
so I picked a spot near a bridge to sit with my inner hecklers.
The birds settled a bit with my stillness. I couldn't help but think
here is my cacophonous mind. My distractability. Yet another
digression. The water in my body is no good for irrigation but still
in the acequia my thoughts eventually became fluid, accepting even
the impulse to rise and stick out my arms, my deciduous branches.

LXXİV.

The other night it occurred to me that if I were to start rattling
off the numbers for pi now, I wouldn't need to round up until
my last exhalation. At the time, the proposition held promise.
Potentially my mind could succumb to the kind of focus required
for such rote calculations. Granted that'd only get me a finite slice
of the infinite, but that's a lot. For a moment I envisioned solace.
3.14 or John 3:16, I'd like to find purpose, some work I can follow
through to the end. I botch things. It frightens me into believing
I wouldn't mind dying here, in this poem. If the rest of my life
consisted of simply fourteen lines, I believe I could do it well.
Any longer and I am less certain I can maintain this controlled
floundering. I picture myself perpetually flopping about. Desire
to live rivals my desire for certainty. I want to cling and I want
to let go. I want to cross my fingers and see what comes next.

LXXV.

Twinkle twinkle I saw stars again. No cloud in the sky can
come between me and perception of an unreal constellation
in the lower hemisphere of my vision. The fierce shine, pure
flicker despite midday sun, was devastating. Visual sirens.
I forgot my aching shoulder, my last sin, the ongoing count
of friend, lost friend. The only responsibility I felt right then
was to stay with the fleeting. I could have cared less what
the real back drop was. To love against logic seems comic
or reprehensible. To love like that is to glimpse the dream
inside my dreams. The fading left me wistful, left me world-
curious as if the glimmerings were promises sealed between
my conscious mind and this old body: *seven sisters, fifteen
pomegranate seeds, teeth of a lion, there will be brightness
beyond your control.* Something inside this husk shines.

LXXVI.

What am I going to do with my frailty? I cannot get around
weakness any more than I can forget my knees. So I have this
and that, a rice paper skeleton and origami heart. The tss,tss
steady rip in my consciousness gets to the bottom of things not
unlike a day laborer with a good shovel. Someday I will be more
than an ostrich, head plunged into sand. One burial or the other
makes me flinch. My bitten tongue aches. Paradoxically I'm tired
of listening to the yammering of my bigger mouth, with its neuro-
chemical tongue lashings and synaptical beratings. What if maybe
I bring this creaking awkwardness into full sun, then go to my bed
rocking my own fragilities gently, create a slingshot (or a mindset)
with enough elasticity to tap the weight of each shortcoming and
fling me: panorama of green ribbon, ruddy band, sand and sand-
stone plus high in a tree, the smallest nest, cracked shell, crook'd.

LXXVii.

This year my body has taken forms ranging from bystander
at my own life to a pile of molecules arghing. When my cat
sleeps curled beside me, I realize my flesh is getting round
again. As the convex line of her spine fits the concave curve
of my side, all points making contact, I remember my body
as something efficient and this is pleasurable. I even rake
these days, my shoulder having resumed its place at the top
of my arm, pain tossed to the moths with my winter garments.
If I can carry 50 pounds of cracked corn today, I won't forget
that when I couldn't, friends shouldered the task as soon as
I mustered enough gumption to get around the stubbornest ox
in my brain (my desire for self sufficiency) and ask. Healing
I look forward to interactions not motivated by need. I need
interactions. Desperation made me brave, left me envisioning.

LXXViii.

Why must people insist on such inordinate kindness? Whenever
I think I've got inhumanity figured out and am ready to relinquish
my own compassion and codify hostility, a single act reduces me
to vision. Simple things: small talk and a strawberry at a party
where I am sober and unspringing against the wall, a book written
by one person and mailed by another, a letter sent from Nicaragua,
hands that don't touch me, one or two that do. Then, oh the guilt
when I peruse my mindfill. And not because I need to be productive
or am unwilling to fritter time, rather because my past is littered
with violence. I hope one day I'll wake up and be done contemplating
suicide, but the history of the world and my thinking precludes that.
In the context of so much cruelty, when at times the only vindication
for an abuse of power or intimacy is to bleed very well, any closure
could be welcome, but this openness, this possibility, is ferocious.

LXXIX.

I have to think and live small. Earlier I was nearly blinded
when the belly of a pheasant struck full sun. I live by this bird,
know it's strut and ha-hark to flapping, even know iridescence
or thought I did until unexpected glare bowled me over. Suddenly
alfalfa was rising fast, or I was falling, casting about for a limb
of the overhanging cottonwood, missing, my six feet floundering,
in and out of the furrows, delirious and green, I gave myself up
to awe, dropped kerplunk down splayed in the first available rut
and looked up, thinking, I will pay for this, looked up, expecting
death or a turkey vulture, instead through branches I saw in the sky
a pair of ducks. Leave me here, quacking. Forever even. I'll be okay.
If this entire city is reduced to an acre of alfalfa, the trailer to its
broken window, my body to a spine crunkled on dirt, I'll be okay.
Soon the tree will green up and obscure one beauty with another.

LXXX.

Lymph nodes with delusions of grandeur make an impression
on my nervous system, my right leg is hot on the press. So I limb
along, emanating heat, with fantasies of encountering someone
frostbitten who might appreciate my warmth. Many are cold
but few will embrace much of anything. No form of existence
lacks merit. Some of us know this. Not everyone will live long
enough or be exposed enough to experience the second coming
of chickenpox. I did, and now that eternity has passed, I'm glad.
What's skin deep has been exposed as such and pain sheers life
down to bare essence. Here in Pariahville, I'm finally unshackled
from proper sensibilities. After just three days and three nights
I resigned myself to whatever: toss this body out a window, or
get a cane, braids, and shawl. Trekking to the phone was enough
to relearn what politeness is not worth and what empathy is.

LXXXi.

Midnight my chickens set up such a ruckus that I lock the door
behind me and traipse barefoot on out to the coop with a hammer.
My rooster is audibly calmed by my presence, and I'm pleased
that somewhere in a bird's brain, I am associated with goodness,
maybe corn and table scraps, and now, in duress with safety. Then
I doubt. My dog is barking in the trailer and I feel inconsequential
weight in my hand. I'd grabbed the first available wieldable, not
even my framing hammer, not even the flashlight. And in the dark
I wonder what I thought I was gonna do, then do what makes sense.
I listen. And when I hear an unfeathered thump in the coop, I try
calling it by name: *possum? skunk? beelzebub?* My voice, even
inflected with fear and curiosity, is effective. Streak of a ghost, not
coyote, not cat, an ermine disappears under the fence before I can. . .
anything. So I search for, and find, my displaced hen, put her back.

LXXXII.

One day I will do like St. Francis and apologize to my body
but not yet. I'm not ready. If it's been a decade since I woke up
and remembered to feel pain only upon sitting down across town
and finding holes half an inch deep in both my heels where nails
from the shoes I'd ground into pavement all night rose up, and if
it's been almost as long since I ceased carrying around a matchbook
with a razor tucked inside *just in case*, if I've survived to abandon
those techniques of unintentional mindlessness and intentional acts
to shift or get focus, now I'm confounded because I'm grateful, and
I worry I'll forget this. When my mood changes, I'm liable to dismiss
my own fonder memories like naughty schoolchildren unless I can't
ignore some tangible. So if I didn't crawl on my knees for 100 miles
repenting, I did walk, my backpack filled with books, a good one
on Chimayo's history and a Bible. 89 miles for muscle memory.

LXXXiii.

The veil is lifted. In the Kunduz market a woman trying to speak
is poked with a stick and tapestries are rolled back to expose soft
porn. *First things first,* I think. Later on the radio, I hear a woman
from Afghanistan demand equal representation from a platform
in Amsterdam. Her voice is clear, convictions strong. I find myself
nodding *yes,* my sweet familiar, then shaking my head, *no,* my un-
recognizable. The thought *legitimate but absurd,* forces me to face
my own burkha: deep compromise. Abstractions blur into realities.
I notice old bruises on my thighs shaped like tokens for video games
and wonder how this happened. Rohipnal? Things always go back-
wards. Once on a date set up for rape, *no* was failing, so I proposed
I pick the guy up, carry *him* over the threshold. When he said *yes,*
I hauled him downstairs, dropped him, and ran. I got lucky. This town,
unlike Juarez, has no late buses running from *maquin-a-dormir* to grave.

LXXXİV.

My friend calls to me from the middle of the Pacific Ocean. "Hey,"
first syllable and I'm right there, lifted out of the trailer, and "you"
plunk down beside him, but as conversation drifts back to desert,
a dust devil hits the great water in my head. I struggle to hang on,
ride the vocalized crest of what's been happening here. Most people
would miss (or prefer to ignore) the moment my mouth begins going
forwards and backwards at the same time, when I confess difficulty
"but" begin lashing my sentences to "fine." Not him though. He speaks
my language. I don't mean English, Greek or Hungarian, nothing literal,
rather whatever leaps the gap between the said and unsaid, a resonance
so deep, neurological empathy must be centuries old. With four words,
"Let it," he caught me "get" in a net, and "better" lifted me (gasp) out
of chagrin into gratitude—I don't have to resist everything or even do
much of anything except breathe my way across these sound barriers.

LXXXV.

Oh Thomas. I had hoped to get closer to you, to find myself
balanced on a one-legged stool eating rice and dandelion greens
with acumen, to look up one day and see order in the trailer, but
my copy of the Benedictine Rule is simply shelved (if read) next
to your books, borrowed or bought, not even the whole collection.
And what did I think would happen? Men with good libraries still
whine for blow jobs. Women, whether we become students or dust,
often end up driven primarily to become thin as a subplot, or worse
a pressed flower, just to fit in somewhere. Reading, writing, mopping.
For over two years—life always jutting in—I've tried but these letters
barely scratch the topsoil of your grave. I mope. Meanwhile the light
fixture has fallen from the wall above the bathroom sink and dangles
so that the bare bulb knocks against the mirror, the pull chain against
the bulb, getting hot. Just know: it's bright and I think of you often.

LXXXVI.

In a dream I brew tea for a neighbor. He arrives unexpectedly

so I hurry to apologize for the mess and offer what I can: licorice

peach ginger hibiscus? He seems confused as if by the myriad teas,

which truthfully have startled me, my cupboards a sudden wealth

of aroma and choice. Then he says, *I hadn't envisioned the door.*

I put the kettle on, look back over my shoulder. Did he think I lived

totally encapsulated by tin? Shut-in? I do sometimes but officially

the door works. I look at it. Oh yeah, it is super-shabby. I'd forgotten

all the cracks in the pane of glass. A person can get used to anything.

Besides, for me the shatter pattern is visible proof of invisible forces.

I hand him his tea in a peanutbutter jar, then tell him how I'd opened

the door and the wind ripped it from my hand. Wham. I'm dreaming.

Awake, I drink tea alone. He'd only showed up because I fell asleep

and forgot to be embarrassed or even wondering if I ought to be.

LXXXVİİ.

All things are relative. When I go to the hospital to see my friend,
I arrive in time inversely proportional to the grief I felt for delaying
seeing my grandma. Expedited. I bring him gifts to make her laugh
but he's still happy to see me, and the IV is bubbling steadily onward.
So I sit bedside, listen to his stories, read about upcoming procedures.
The next day tubes stick from his lungs draining fluid the color of ripe
watermelon into a machine, his own personal waterfountain, a gurgling
feng shui arrangement. The oxygen tube slips sideways and his gown
won't stay up but it's okay. His ribs are my grandma's hairpins, catch
the cloth as it drops. I am happy here against his shins. I like the way
my grandmother's face looked so young, high cheekboned, whenever
she took her teeth out. I'm glad I got to kiss her to sleep even if I hear
fear in my friend's voice. When grandma was sick, I wouldn't watch
the northern lights even, because I knew they'd flicker and be gone.

LXXXVĪĪĪ.

A buddhist down the road wields a hatchet. I left my chainsaw
back at the trailer so I approach warily though all I want is sugar
or was it gasoline, maybe something less tangible? I forget, figure
perhaps I'll remember when my mind (which comes tumbling after
my feet) catches up. This quiet is aftermath. Last night winds beat
down, ripping up anything with an inclination to fly into the sky.
All the connective tissue in the community is bruised, fences and
such. In my own yard, my dead tree with its three birdfeeders fell
onto the new garden or would have except it was caught by the roof
of the shed and my fence. My neighbor is calm. I ask, *Did you call?*
He volunteers nothing, but no air on the prowl is ever insubstantial.
Did you call the wind? I see his fence is downed. *Did you call the wind
unkind for prying at the edges of everything?* He says, *Now I have kindling.*
Later I call a friend to come play catch the logs, spare the seedlings.

LXXXiX.

When conversation dwindled, the man beside me hoisted a rock
out of the earth and set it to the side. Then he said, softly, *Look.*
If he wanted to make an impression on me, he did, contemplating
patterns ground in soil, an exposed root, pale insects. We sat round
that quiet flirtation as if we wished intimacy could be achieved so
simply or believed that closeness was always an uplifting experience.
In the mountains, my neighbor would lay out cardboard in the sun.
Pick up that and you'd find rattlers. Some things shouldn't happen
too fast. Yet, clothes get cast aside and skin explored as if our scars
will once-upon-a-time all the necessary anecdotes but flesh isn't real
dirt. We remain hidden, often shamed, wishing people understood
how paths get carved against obstacles and even a regular old stone's
oppression can block light until deprivation eclipses everything else.
Inevitably, most of us will end up climbing the walls like centipedes.

XC.

He said, "You're *nuckin' futƺ.*" I said, "*Amulok, bambooƺulok*. A fair
in Mexico doesn't sound good?" I only wanted a little consideration
for my plan. A woman shouldn't have to live without room for her
own whims to be expressed. Responding *yes* or *no* is quite adequate.
Carousels will keep going round no matter who can't hear the music.
I ride plenty. I ride always. Dark, light, the circumference of the moon.
I wouldn't subject another person to much, but on the rising cycle, after
desolation, the bleak-bleak-gritty-gritty, I can't resist barking, in hopes
someone will pony up, hike at midnight, staple cloth to telephone poles,
or head for the Mississippi because it's the Mississippi. That's logical.
Once I carried a twenty foot whip of seaweed through airline terminals,
kept it in my bathtub for a week, so I could show desert friends *ocean*.
I do what I can, when I can, with or without other people. Once a horse
showed some initiative, *pushing me* into the water tank I was fixing.

XCI.

It's fire season but I know too many people who'd refuse to spit
on a spark this drought just to protect some ideal of independence,
as if compassion beyond self or nuclear affiliates belies weakness.
Oh well, I'm broke and I menstruate. I break many great American
taboos daily and kindness will I hope be a mainstay despite being
a source of mockery. Nonetheless Thomas, I'm searching for better
outlets than the stage or the pocket of an individual off to get a fix.
Caring and knowing how to express it can be two different things.
I've witnessed trances come over my rather stern and sensible father
then wham he'd buy a truck on credit cards and give it to strangers.
Nonetheless even he becomes more discerning. Last time he rented
an apartment to a woman with no money, he understood that as soon
as her face healed up from the beating her boyfriend had given her,
she'd be able to get tips again at the restaurant. That made sense.

XCII.

Half moon, dark sky. I gaze at the diameter, the line that is cusp
between visible light and not visible light. Once, sitting in the booth
across from me, a friend with faith said, *El que nace pa tamalero
hasta del cielo le caen las ojas,* then translated, *If you're meant to
make tamales, the corn husks will even fall from the sky*. Funny,
I believe him. On my odd pilgrimage, I found three pairs of high-heel
dance shoes lined up neatly beside the highway, and yet he's the one
with the wife and two daughters who study flamenco. Their duende
is strong, touches me. I cherish all my vicarious family lives, wish
I could have my own goat, never got sick, could handle the milking
by myself. Someone else's grandma sent word back from Michigan,
Tell her she's not alone. I don't know what I am. Lucky? Blessed?
A woman who cannot even make posole looking at a halved moon
with nothing falling on her? No petals or pianos, no cumbersomes.

XCIII.

I am no seer, Thomas. My vision does the usual selective service,
whereby we isolate the world-parts we want to look at, draft black-
n-blue prints of the chosen reality in our minds, then simplify that
into something black-n-white and over-pat, and think it's done soon
as we get the newspaper, this book, that contract, the cup of coffee
with cream. Even so, my eyes are tired, cried out, pent in my skull,
and I am only a small woman whose mind latches on small things—
like a man saying that his brother (killed by friendly fire) was always
a paintball aficionado, or how "short or long sleeves?" can translate
into *mal*, "how to shop," or *torture*, "where to chop." I notice bombings
in Bethlehem because of alliteration. It's nothing. Yesterday a local
faced a real inferno down his road and thought he'd created hell. Pride
is a tragic flaw. He accidentally lit up Peñasco then killed himself, giving
no credit to tobacco companies, sprawl, global warming, the rest of us.

XCIV.

Trees, even blossoming violently, don't make me think of crucifixion
but rather of sitting, resting in the shade, until a kind of enlightenment
falls upon me, or at least I understand gravity. Today though, I simply
hurt, an attachment here, lack of nourishment there, suspect untended
wounds contain seeds for every unkindness ever perpetrated. Before
I lash out anymore, I'd like to find a way to assuage my grief. So I sit,
try to make a poultice under salt cedar. I resonate with this unwanted
tree, even if I never promised flood control, even if I don't propagate,
or dry up the Rio Grande. I've been uprooted and re-rooted almost as
thoughtlessly and more often. If I feel displaced not by geography but
by who I am in the context of status quo, still I know the river's edge,
know harangued by bulldozers, fear the kind of goats that'd chew up
the only page where I've got space to breathe. That I'm not alone helps
me to speak. Plus, wildly, needles on salt cedar remind me of gauze.

XCV.

I say the smallest of my truths and people respond as if my mouth
emerged from a trenchcoat. I've been flashed before so I recognize
the expression on their faces as what I felt on mine that first time.
Then too often, they just turn away. I am left watching their backs
and this protects them, even linguistically, from being exposed to
an *other* reality. It's an implicit universal concurrence so I cover up,
until impulse, necessity, or lack of (oops) shame, gets the upperhand
and I speak. I cannot believe that all forms of revelation merit horror.
(Context counts.) Ignorance may be bliss but it's not safe or humane.
To be perceived as an affront hurts, encourages my desire to wire
my jaw shut. I remember how St. Augustine wanted to circumcise
his tongue in order to get closer to God. Maybe he got *the look* and
decided to transform the metaphor. Unlikely but certainly his work
fostered my desire to let the monster in my mouth become ecstatic.

XCVİ.

In a dream I saw myself undressing and learned how to be a nun
for a few seconds every day. I was already in the habit of wearing
t-shirts. Now whenever I pull one off, over my head, I stop right
as the collar crests my brow, then *feel* what I look like, with my hair
bound back in cloth, my face ringed and calm. Then my (nearly) nude
torso makes me laugh. Which is good. Playfulness is divine. As for
the other *none*, I need work. I spent a week polishing my mirror until
it was a mirror. Now I see that when I'm rotten jittering, my body can
remain calm. If the discrepancy disturbs me, it also heartens me, stills
the jitters. Just give me time Thomas, a bit more. I won't waste all of it.
I'm too happy. There are moments I love, when I believe *gruesome*
can be transformed into *some grew*. The phrase *needling each other*
took a whole new slant when I started acupuncture after the accident,
pointed me in *for* directions. Now I'm a golden rooster on one leg.

XCVII.

I need you to know I can be all over the page. The fact that I count
to fourteen is merely a struggle to hold my temper. Ten's not enough.
The rigor seems constricting but actually I live with less prescriptions
than when I began this. And I'm not trying to withhold any absurdity.
Between these lines I can't even stand up straight (though at times I do
flatten out to sleep). Not so long ago, I taught *Experiencing the Arts*
three hours after going bankrupt. I only read poems from Chapter 7.
Last week, I thought I was headed for prison. I wasn't. This just shows
the irrelevance of what I think. Still, I learn from mundane felix culpas,
make peace with breaking down. It helps to have been praised for demo-
lition. The job took me two hours but the client had taken a swing at it
on and off for two weeks and failed. He just lacked faith. I knew that
each strike where nothing seems to happen leads to the one that crashes
everything. I was simply persistent and perhaps knowing where to hit.

XCVIII.

When my grandfather died, I mourned him well, in North Dakota
in a field, singing. Fourteen years later when grandma died I couldn't
even speak; a cousin had to read my poem for her memorial. Originally
we'd become close because we loved the same man. For years our lives
revolved around grandpa's cancer. When he passed, she threw a vase
of flowers across the room because my uncle wouldn't trim his handlebar
moustache for the funeral. That day she and I started over from scratch,
learning each other, awkwardly, both still growing up. During her youth,
she'd been taunted, called *squaw*. When she was eighty, I learned that
she still felt the pang of racism. Still defensive, she called herself *dark-
skinned Norwegian*. Doors kept opening into rolled model T's, piano
recitals, vacuum cleaners, history. In the 20's she won $25 for *How to
Keep the Boys and Girls on the Farm*. Her essay predates the demise of
family farms. Now everybody knows you can't keep the boys and girls.

XCIX.

Your love's here. I look up, quietly startled, as if the elm's discreet.
What got my attention was not a solitary tap, but an accumulation
of tapping. When I look back at my typewriter, I see a small beetle
maneuvering slowly across the keys as if the alphabet was a strange
landscape. This bug's just a loner, season's first. Later I'll drape cloth
over the machine to keep all kinds of insect life from slipping into
the abyss. I don't mind that I am not alone in my desire to live here.
I get to eat my eggs before they hatch, and sometimes when I wash
dishes, cows moo longingly across the fence. An escaped one kicked
over my statue of Francis. I was impressed that a contemporary cow
would know which saint to pester about domestication. It's good here.
Slowly feral. The elm's taking decades to crunch in the kitchen wall.
At the far end of the trailer, new blossoms cling between screen and
slatted window glass. It's actually a locust that pokes into my study.

C.

Things get lost and found in translation. Attempts in any language
to write, or even to speak, muck up the original impulse and risk
a lucky discovery. My tongue can break any language. I spent years
asking people (in English) if they knew the German word for *taking
a step back, better to leap forward*. Turns out to be French, a phrase
of Jung's, *reculer pour mieux sauter*. I needed it but I can't explain why.
To extricate ideas from the brambles of Americana? To thrust languages
into my ears that I've not yet heard misused? Maybe. Lately I'm studying
Chinese. A Taiwanese man told me *zizijiao* means the cry of a monkey.
A woman from Beijing claims it's the cry of a bird that only sounds like
a monkey. Here in Alameda, I suspect *zizijiao* means the cry of a girl
who'd prefer to be a bird or a monkey but can't. So she contemplates
sandpipers, hoping at least to figure out how to move when moving,
and how to be still when still, body mind and tongue consensual.

Colophon

Set in Monotype Fournier (1925) based on the
typeface "St Augustin Ordinaire" cut by
Pierre Simon Fournier in 1740. Innovative and
prolific, Fournier developed the idea of a type
family, introduced an early version of the "point"
system, and through his foundry created over
100 alphabets of his own design. He was also adept
in the creation and use of typographic ornaments
then known as "little flowers." This version of
his work shows the slightly accentuated sharpness
of the Neoclassical style which "holds the
middle course between charm & utility."

•

Book design by J.B. Bryan

Lisa Gill has performed in the Albuquerque Poetry Festival,
the Taos Poetry Circus, the Seattle Poetry Festival, Zerxfest
and twice been part of the Thomas McGrath Visiting Writers
Series at Moorhead State University in Minnesota. Her short
story "Holding Zeno's Suitcase in Kansas, Flowering" was
selected for first place in the 7th edition of *American Fiction* and
nominated for a Pushcart Prize. She's taught the Ethics and
Methodology of Guerilla Literature and has recently been working
with Na-Da (Not A Disco Act), a multi-disciplinary artists'
collaborative. She has also built barns, laid bricks, waited tables,
counted cans in supermarkets, and peeled green chile on the clock.
She is currently at work on a collection for New Rivers Press and
has begun preliminary studies in the field of Chinese medicine.
Red as a Lotus is her first book.

Index of First Lines

25 ❋ Church on Sundays was standard when I was a child but

26 ❋ One of my grandmothers got caught reading the newspaper

27 ❋ The month I tried following the liturgy of the hours, I was

28 ❋ The sky was heavy today, Thomas. By noon I'd made good

29 ❋ When I placed a stone on my tongue, a friend told me

30 ❋ Right now I am in rapture. Winter has a way of putting us

31 ❋ Every day I walk by the ditch. It's a real ditch and a metaphor.

32 ❋ I invited you for rice and asparagus but you stood me up.

33 ❋ When I moved out, I inherited the family Bible. I've had it years

34 ❋ I have lived half my life in the desert. My spine is bleached

35 ❋ At the laundromat, I remember humility. This load's not even

36 ❋ I am not as messed up as I think, nor am I any less flawed than

37 ❋ Down at the adobe pit off Edith, the old anglo has forgotten

38 ❋ I am all wound up. If you give a good tug on the end of the line

39 ❋ A ring-necked pheasant scuttles into brush and my vision wanders

40 ❋ It's the middle of the night, the sky is all creased and no wind

41 ❋ Last week I had an intuition that someone I knew might

42 ❋ One of my friends has a small farm. The first time I dropped by,

43 ❋ A decade ago I tried to sell vacuum cleaners door to door.

44 ❋ I got a splinter imbedded in my thumb when I was working

45 ❋ Yesterday the sky filled with petroleum. On the ground,

46 ❋ Here is sweetness: I can't lick my fingers clean this dusk.

47 ❋ Somewhere in the community a person is belligerent, defensive,

48 ❋ My dog always finds bones in the alfalfa field. I am used

49 ❋ I spent the morning mythed. I pushed a truck up a gravel drive

50 ❋ I hit the road as if it were a linear place to shake my fist.

51 ❋ Rock, burr, shard, I have stepped on many things where I saw

52 ❋ At the start of World War II, there was no word for *bomb* in Navajo,

53 ❋ Sometimes you have to clear the way for what comes next

54 ❋ I thought I could tell what's forested from what's not but sometimes

55 ❋ I wake and find the sky opaque, frozen tactile. I am neither

56 ❋ My lips are raw, having made some pilgrimage across a pasture

57 ❋ Here I admit lapse. Thomas, I have called too many valleys

58 ❋ Perhaps I do miss church. My rooster has taken to crowing

59 ❋ I have a garden Thomas. Last year at this time I had food

60 ❋ Before I began this letter, I sat with a pen and pad and practiced

61　❋　What comes to mind here is the word *hogwash,* as if you

62　❋　I've been dropping things, pens to the floor, my morning coffee

63　❋　What Mary told the breadtruck driver in Iowa gives great heart.

64　❋　Between my body and the green mountain, a barbed wire fence.

65　❋　The river that welcomed itself over my grandmother's stoop and

66　❋　The hens like it when I stay up until dawn. Such basic creatures,

67　❋　Saint John of the Cross came after me in a pick-up and hit hard.

68　❋　One of the last things my grandmother and I shared

69　❋　I hope for no electrical fire in this old trailer. I don't intend

70　❋　In the crash, my windshield miraculously only sustained cracks.

71　❋　I am not unfamiliar with this state. Almost 20 years living

72　❋　With every fall comes flapping. Birds migrate and now flags—

73　❋　In the hospital everyone is patient with the shocked, a certain loss

74　❋　I am neither that far off the tracks nor am I particularly close

75　❋　I sit anchored on my stoop bereft of all things glimmering,

76　❋　The sky is back, looking all starry-eyed. I found it in the desert,

77　❋　This year I made many mistakes that blossomed in the night-

78　❋　I spent the morning casing the mesa for shells. I was struck

79 ✳ Money's tight as a bone girdle. The constriction eases a bit

80 ✳ By the time I woke up and got out of bed, night blanketed

81 ✳ The pregnant co-worker of a daughter of a friend of mine was beaten

82 ✳ Lately I've felt spurned and sore, found myself wanting the world

83 ✳ Twinkle twinkle I saw stars again. No cloud in the sky can

84 ✳ I found a tin can walking the drained ditch, carried it along

85 ✳ The other night it occurred to me that if I were to start rattling

86 ✳ What am I going to do with my frailty? I cannot get around

87 ✳ This year my body has taken forms ranging from bystander

88 ✳ Why must people insist on such inordinate kindness? Whenever

89 ✳ I have to think and live small. Earlier I was nearly blinded

90 ✳ Lymph nodes with delusions of grandeur make an impression

91 ✳ Midnight my chickens set up such a ruckus that I lock the door

92 ✳ One day I will do like St. Francis and apologize to my body

93 ✳ The veil is lifted. In the Kunduz market a woman trying to speak

94 ✳ My friend calls to me from the middle of the Pacific Ocean. "Hey,"

95 ✳ Oh Thomas. I had hoped to get closer to you, to find myself

96 ✳ In a dream I brew tea for a neighbor. He arrives unexpectedly

97 ❋ All things are relative. When I go to the hospital to see my friend,

98 ❋ A buddhist down the road wields a hatchet. I left my chainsaw

99 ❋ When conversation dwindled, the man beside me hoisted a rock

100 ❋ He said, "You're *nuckin' futz*." I said, "*Amulok, bamboozulok*. A fair

101 ❋ It's fire season but I know too many people who'd refuse to spit

102 ❋ Half moon, dark sky. I gaze at the diameter, the line that is cusp

103 ❋ I am no seer, Thomas. My vision does the usual selective service,

104 ❋ Trees, even blossoming violently, don't make me think of crucifixion

105 ❋ I say the smallest of my truths and people respond as if my mouth

106 ❋ In a dream I saw myself undressing and learned how to be a nun

107 ❋ I need you to know I can be all over the page. The fact that I count

108 ❋ When my grandfather died, I mourned him well, in North Dakota

109 ❋ *Your love's here.* I look up, quietly startled, as if the elm's discreet.

110 ❋ Things get lost and found in translation. Attempts in any language